The BRILLIANT BOOK OF EASY RECIPES

The BRILLIANT BOOK OF EASY RECIPES

Susannah Blake

WAYLAND

WAYLAND

Published in paperback in 2014 by Wayland
Copyright © Wayland 2014

Wayland
338 Euston Road
London NW1 3BH

Wayland
Level 17/207 Kent Street
Sydney NSW 2000

All rights reserved
Senior editors: Jennifer Schofield
  and Victoria Brooker
Designers: Lisa Peacock and
  Basement68
Photographer: Andy Crawford

The author and publisher would like to thank
the following models: Jade Campbell, Adam
Menditta, Harriet Couch, Demi Mensah, Robert
Kilminster, Aneesa Qureshi, Kaine Zachary
Levy, Emel Augustin. Taylor Fulton, Ammar
Duffus, Claire Shanahan.

The recipes in this book are
designed to be made by children.
However, we recommend adult
supervision at all times as the
Publisher cannot be held
responsible for any injury caused
while making these recipes.

Some of the material in this book
appeared in the 'Make and Eat'
series, also published by Wayland.

All photographs Andy Crawford
except page 4: Kevin
Fleming/Corbis; page 5 Marie Dubrac/
ANYONE/Getty images (from biscuits); p41
bottom travellight/shutterstock.

Blake, Susannah.
    The brilliant book of easy recipes.
    1. Cooking--Juvenile literature.
    I. Title II. Easy recipes
    641.5-dc23

ISBN: 978 0 7502 8303 8

Printed in China

10 9 8 7 6 5 4 3 2 1

Wayland is a division of
Hachette Children's Books,
an Hachette UK company.
www.hachette.co.uk

Contents

Before you begin

These easy-to-follow, step-by-step instructions will show you how to make some delicious things to eat. From sandwiches and snacks to cakes and biscuits, impress your friends and family with these tasty treats. But before you start cooking, here are some important things you ought to know.

Be prepared

Make sure you have the ingredients you need for the recipe. You don't want to get half way through cooking to find you're missing an ingredient. Check you have all cookery equipment that you need, for example, the right utensils, pots and pans, or paper cases and greaseproof paper.

Measurements

These abbreviations have been used in this book:
- tbsp — tablespoon
- tsp — teaspoon
- ml — millilitre
- g — gram
- l — litre

All eggs are medium unless stated.

Oven temperature

Always ask an adult to turn the oven on for you and to help you put things in the oven. Don't open the oven door while things are cooking or they might not cook as well as they should.

To work out where the cooker dial needs to be for high, medium and low heat, count the marks on the dial and divide it by three. The top third is high and the bottom third is low. The in-between third is medium. Ovens should be preheated to the specified temperature. If you are using a fan-assisted oven, follow the manufacturer's instructions for adjusting the time and temperature.

Cleaning up afterwards

It's not fun, but it has to be done! Make sure you wash up all of the utensils, bowls and saucepans that you've used and wipe up any surfaces.

Health and safety tips

1. Clean all your work surfaces before you start cooking.
2. Tie back long hair away from your face.
3. Wash your hands well with soap and warm water before you start to cook. Wash them after handling any raw meat, poultry or fish.
4. Read through the recipe you are cooking before you start. Check that you have all the equipment and ingredients that you will need.
5. Check the sell-by dates on all food.
6. Wash all fruit and vegetables under cold running water.

7. When preparing food, keep it out of the refrigerator for the shortest time possible. Generally, you should not leave food out of the fridge for more than two hours.
8. Use a different chopping board and knife to prepare meat, chicken and fish from the one you use for preparing fruit and vegetables.
9. Never serve undercooked food, ensure that any meat, fish and chicken is cooked all the way through.
10. Replace used tea towels regularly with clean, dry ones to avoid the spreading of bacteria.

Cookery Equipment

Most of the equipment used in this book can be found at home already. Here are some of the things that you will need in this book:

Baking sheets

Metal sheets for baking food in the oven.

Baking tins

These come in all shapes and sizes so you can bake different shaped loaves and cakes.

Box grater

Use to grate food such as cheese and carrots. Keep your fingers away from the sharp edges.

Bun trays

These come in different sizes and are good for baking cupcakes and muffins.

Chopping boards

These protect your work surface. Make sure you always use a different one for meat and a different one for vegetables.

Colander

Use colanders over the sink, either for washing fruit and vegetables or for draining pasta and cooked vegetables.

Cutters

These come in many different shapes and sizes. Use them to cut out rolled dough.

Frying pan

Use this flat pan to fry vegetables or eggs. You will need to add very little butter or oil to a non-stick pan.

Knives

Be careful when chopping and always keep your fingers away from the sharp blade.

Ladle

Scoop soup into bowls using a ladle.

Measuring cups

These are used just like measuring spoons but for measuring bigger quantities of ingredients.

Measuring jug

Use this to measure liquids and dry ingredients.

Measuring spoons

Measuring spoons help you to use the exact amount of ingredients.

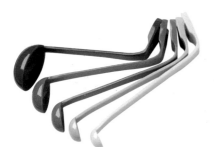

Pastry brush

Use to brush marinades and oil onto foods.

Plastic spatula

These are great for scraping mixtures, such as dips, from the sides of bowls.

Roasting tray

Use to roast meat and vegetables in the oven.

Rolling pin

Round wooden rolling pins can be used to roll out bread and pizza dough.

Scales

Use scales to measure dry and solid ingredients accurately.

Sieve

These may be small, medium or large and are useful for sifting flour and icing sugar.

Slotted spoon

This spoon is useful for taking solid food out of liquids as the liquid drains through the holes.

Wire rack

Breads and cakes should always be cooled on a rack to allow air to circulate underneath.

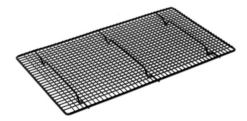

Wooden spatulas

Flat-ended spatulas are good for scraping foods such as scrambled eggs from the bottom of a pan.

Wooden spoons

Use these spoons to stir food when cooking or to mix batters and dough when making bread.

Bread
and
Pizza

14

Contents

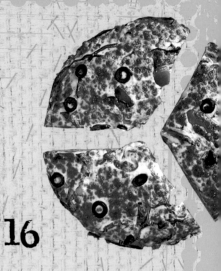

All about bread and pizza

People have eaten bread for thousands of years. Loaves have been found in ancient Egyptian tombs that are over 5,000 years old. Today, there are many kinds of bread from all over the world, and the same dough that is used to make bread can also be used to make pizza.

Making dough

Bread dough is usually made from four ingredients – flour; a leavening ingredient, such as yeast, to make it rise; salt and a liquid, such as water. The flour used to make dough usually comes from ground wheat but flour from other grains, such as rye and corn, can also be used.

Kneading dough

Before baking it to make bread, dough must be kneaded. To knead dough, sprinkle some flour onto your work surface then turn the dough out on to the surface. Using the heel of your hands, press down on the dough to flatten it. Fold the dough over into a ball shape and press it again with the heel of your hand. Continue pressing and folding, trying to end up with the dough in a ball shape each time. This basic dough can be made into rounds to make pizzas or shaped into loaves or rolls. Extra ingredients, such as dried fruit and herbs, can be added to give the bread a unique flavour.

Bread from around the world

There are hundreds of different types of bread from around the world. They are made from different combinations of the basic ingredients and are cooked in different ways to produce their unique shape, taste and texture. Classic breads include Indian naan, which is a flattish, oval-shaped bread cooked on a griddle. The Jewish bagel is a ring-shaped roll — the dough is shaped, then boiled or steamed before baking to give it a chewy texture. The French stick is a white, crusty loaf that can be large or small. Caribbean buns are a dense, spicy teabread flavoured with molasses and studded with dried fruit.

Get started

In this chapter you can learn to make all kinds of bread and pizza. All the recipes use everyday kitchen equipment, such as knives, spoons, forks and chopping boards. You can see pictures of the different equipment that you may need on pages 8–11. Before you start, check that you have all the equipment that you will need and make a list of any ingredients that you need to buy. Make sure that there is an adult to help you, especially with the recipes that involve using the cooker or oven. When you have everything you need, make sure all the kitchen surfaces are clean and wash your hands well with soap and water. If you have long hair, tie it back. Always wash raw fruits and vegetables under cold running water before preparing or cooking them. This will help to remove any dirt and germs. Then, put on an apron and get cooking!

Soda bread

You will need

For 1 loaf:
- 40g butter, plus extra for greasing
- 225g wholemeal flour, plus extra for dusting · 225g plain white flour
- 1 tsp salt · 2 tsp bicarbonate of soda
- 2 tsp cream of tartar · 1 tsp caster sugar
- 175ml milk ·175ml plain yogurt

Extra equipment

· baking sheet · wire rack · sieve
Ask an adult to help you use the oven

Breads leavened using yeast need to be left to rise. This traditional Irish bread uses bicarbonate of soda and cream of tartar instead of yeast, so it can be put straight in the oven.

1. Preheat the oven to 190°C/375°F/Gas 5. Rub a little butter over the baking sheet to coat it.

2. Hold the sieve over a bowl and pour the wholemeal and white flours, salt, bicarbonate of soda and cream of tartar into it. Tap the side of the sieve until the ingredients have fallen into the bowl below.

3. Cut the butter into small pieces, then add them to the flour mixture.

4. Rub the butter into the flour until the mixture looks like breadcrumbs. Stir in the sugar.

5. Make a well in the middle of the flour crumbs. Mix the milk and yogurt together and pour the mixture into the well. Stir to make a soft dough. If the dough is dry, add a dribble more milk. If the mixture is too wet, add a sprinkle more flour.

6. Sprinkle a little flour over your work surface. Turn the dough onto the work surface and shape it into a round shape.

7. Place the round on a baking sheet and, with a sharp knife, mark a cross in the top of the loaf. Cut quite deep into the dough, but not all the way through.

8. Sprinkle a little more flour over the top of the loaf and put it in the oven. Bake it for about 40 minutes until well risen.

9. When the loaf is cooked, put it on a wire rack to cool. Serve it warm with butter.

Is it cooked?

To check if bread is cooked, use oven gloves to take the loaf out of the oven. Holding the loaf in a gloved hand, remove the other glove and tap the base of the loaf. It should sound hollow if it is cooked through. If it is not cooked, put the loaf in the oven for a few more minutes then check it again.

Corn bread

This bread is made using cornmeal. The cornmeal gives the bread a lovely yellow colour and a distinctive taste. Baking powder makes this bread rise.

You will need
For 1 loaf:
- 4 tbsp sunflower oil, plus extra for greasing · 175g cornmeal
- 115g plain flour · 1 tbsp caster sugar
- 1/4 tsp salt · 1 tbsp baking powder
- 2 eggs ·150ml milk · 125ml plain yogurt

Extra equipment
- 20cm square cake tin · metal skewer
Ask an adult to help you use the oven.

1. Preheat the oven to 200°C/400°F/Gas 6. Rub a little oil inside the cake tin, making sure the surfaces are coated all over.

2. Put the cornmeal, flour, sugar, salt and baking powder in a bowl. Mix them together and make a well in the middle of the mixture. Set aside for later.

3. Break the eggs into another bowl and beat them with a fork. Add the milk, yogurt and sunflower oil and stir.

4. Pour the egg mixture into the well in the cornmeal. Stir the ingredients together, bringing the dry ingredients into the middle of the bowl.

Amazing maize

Cornmeal is made from maize, which is a major crop in the southern states of the United States. Bread made from cornmeal is very popular there and is served as an accompaniment to dishes such as fried chicken. It is also used as the base for turkey stuffing.

5. Pour the mixture into the tin. Make sure it goes into the corners of the tin. Bake the bread for about 25 minutes until it is firm and golden.

6. To check if the bread is cooked, press a skewer into the middle, then gently pull it out. If it comes out clean, the corn bread is cooked. If there are still crumbs on the skewer, put the bread back in the oven for a few more minutes.

7. When the bread is cooked, remove the tin from the oven and put it on a heatproof surface. Leave the bread to cool in the tin for about 10 minutes.

8. Wearing an oven mitt, run a knife around the inside edges of the tin to loosen the bread. Hold a board on top of the tin and flip over the board and tin. If you lift off the tin, the bread should come out. Cut the bread into wedges and serve them warm.

Wholemeal bread

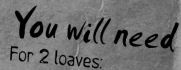

This recipe is based on the recipe for traditional Grant loaves. It is popular because the dough does not need to be kneaded before it is put into tins.

You will need
For 2 loaves:
· oil for greasing · 900g wholemeal bread flour · 2 tsp salt · 800ml warm water · 7g sachet easy-blend dried yeast · 2 tsp muscovado sugar

Extra equipment
· 2 x 2lb loaf tins · sieve · measuring jug · clear film · wire rack
Ask an adult to help you use the oven.

1. Rub a little oil inside each loaf tin, making sure the surface is thoroughly coated. Put the tins in a warm place.

2. Mix the flour and salt together and sieve them into a bowl. Make a well in the centre of the flour mixture. Put the bowl in a warm place.

3. Pour 150ml of warm water into a measuring jug. Check the temperature by putting your finger in the water. It should feel warm to the touch, but not hot. Sprinkle over the yeast and leave it to stand for 1 minute. Then sprinkle over the sugar, stir and leave to stand for 10 minutes.

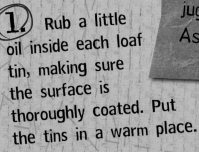

Yeast
Yeast is a type of fungus that grows quickly. As it grows it produces bubbles of carbon dioxide, which make the bread rise. The perfect temperature for yeast to grow in is 38°C. As it is killed in temperatures over 60°C, it is important to check that the water is not too hot before mixing it with the yeast.

4. Pour the yeast mixture into the flour. Measure out another 650ml of warm water. Check the temperature, then pour it into the flour. Stir until the dough is well mixed.

5. Divide the mixture between the two tins, flattening it slightly with the back of a spoon.

6. Tear off two pieces of clear film and rub a little oil on each one. Cover each tin oil side down and put it in a warm place to rise for about 30 minutes, or until the dough has risen by about one-third.

7. While the bread rises, preheat the oven to 200°C/400°F/Gas 6. When the loaves have risen, bake them for about 40 minutes.

8. Following the panel instructions on page 19, check if the bread is cooked. When cooked, turn the loaves out onto a wire rack and leave them to cool.

Cottage loaf

This traditional English loaf has a distinctive shape. It can be made using white or wholemeal flour and is delicious served warm with Cheddar cheese.

You will need

For 1 loaf:
- 575g strong white bread flour, plus extra for dusting · 7g sachet easy-blend dried yeast
- 1 tsp salt · 350ml warm water
- 1 tbsp sunflower oil, plus extra for oiling

Extra equipment

· pastry brush · kitchen scissors · baking sheet · clear film · wire rack
Ask an adult to help you use the oven.

1. Put the flour, yeast and salt in a large bowl and mix them together. Make a well in the middle of the mixture.

2. Check the temperature of the water — it should feel warm, but not hot. Pour the water into the well in the flour and add the oil. Mix to make a rough dough.

3. Sprinkle a little flour onto your work surface, then knead the dough for about 10 minutes until it is smooth and elastic. If the dough is sticky, sprinkle over a little more flour as you knead.

4. Brush a little sunflower oil inside a clean bowl. Put the dough in the bowl, then brush the top with a little oil. Cover the bowl with clear film and leave it to stand in a warm place for 45 minutes, or until it has doubled in size.

5. When it has risen, punch the dough a couple of times to get rid of the air.

Shaping loaves

Bread dough can be shaped into all kinds of loaves before baking: rings, rounds and sticks. Many shapes are specific to countries. In France, the traditional shaped loaf is a baton, or stick. In Italy, there is the flat, dimpled focaccia (see page 26) and the flat, oval or rectangular ciabatta. In regions of Spain and Portugal you will find crusty round loaves.

6. Sprinkle your work surface with a little flour and knead the dough for about 2 minutes. Cut off about one-third of the dough and shape both pieces into round balls.

7. Grease a baking sheet then dust it with flour. Put the larger ball on the sheet and brush it with water. Place the second ball on top. Dip two fingers in flour, then press them down into the middle of the two balls to stick them together. Using kitchen scissors, make little snips around the edge of the top ball.

8. Grease some clear film with oil then use it to cover the dough. Leave the dough to rise in a warm place for 40 minutes.

9. About 15 minutes before the end of the rising time, preheat the oven to 190°C/375°F/Gas 5. Remove the clear film and sprinkle the loaf with a light dusting of flour.

10. Bake the loaf for about 40 minutes until golden brown, then use oven gloves to place it on a wire rack to cool before serving.

Garlic focaccia

This is a classic Italian bread. It can be plain or flavoured with herbs, onions or other ingredients such as sundried tomatoes.

You will need

For two loaves:
· 500g strong white bread flour, plus extra for dusting · 7g sachet of easy-blend dried yeast · 1 tsp salt · 325ml warm water · 6 tsp olive oil · sea salt · 3 garlic cloves, chopped

Extra equipment

· sieve · clear film · rolling pin · 2 x 25cm cake tins or pizza pans · wire rack
Ask an adult to help you use the oven

1. Mix the flour, yeast and salt together, then sieve them into a bowl. Make a well in the middle of the mixture.

2. Check the temperature of the water by putting your finger into it. It should feel just warm, but not hot.

3. Pour the water into the well in the flour and add 3 tsp of olive oil. Stir together to make a soft dough.

The home of Focaccia

Focaccia is particularly associated with Liguria in Italy. This region stretches along the coast in the northwest of the country. Another famous speciality of the region is pesto — a pasta sauce made of basil, pine nuts, garlic and cheese.

4. Sprinkle a little flour over your work surface, then knead the dough for about 10 minutes. If the dough is sticky, continue sprinkling on a little more flour as you work.

5. Wash your hands, then rub a little oil inside a clean bowl. Put the dough inside and pat your oily hands on the dough to make it oily too. Cover the bowl with clear film and leave it to rise in a warm place for 1 hour.

6. When the dough has risen, sprinkle your work surface with a little flour and tip the dough onto it. Press down on the dough to expel some of the air. Divide the dough into two equal pieces, then roll it into two balls. Roll each piece into 25cm rounds and put them inside cake or pizza tins.

7. Cover the tins with clear film and leave to rise in a warm place for about 30 minutes. Meanwhile, preheat the oven to 200°C/400°F/Gas 6.

8. Uncover the tins and poke the dough with your fingertips to make dimples all over the surface. Drizzle over the rest of the olive oil and sprinkle a little sea salt over each one. Sprinkle over the chopped garlic.

9. Bake for 25–30 minutes until the loaves are golden. When they are cooked, use a spatula to lift the loaves from the tins and transfer them to a wire rack. Serve warm.

Fruity buns

These sweet buns are studded with sultanas. They are delicious when eaten warm.

1. Melt the butter over a low heat then set it aside.

2. Combine the flour, yeast, salt, sugar and cinnamon and sieve them into a clean bowl.

3. Stir the sultanas into the flour mixture. Make a well in the middle of the mixture.

5. Fold in the ingredients to make a soft dough. If the dough is a little dry, add a drizzle more water. If it is a little sticky, add a sprinkle more flour.

You will need
For 12 buns:
- 40g butter · 500g strong white bread flour, plus extra for dusting
- 7g sachet easy-blend dried yeast
- 1 tsp salt · 3 tbsp caster sugar
- 1 tsp ground cinnamon
- 175g sultanas · 275ml warm water
- sunflower oil · milk, for brushing

Extra equipment
- sieve · clear film · baking sheet
- pastry brush · wire rack

Ask an adult to help you use the oven.

4. Check the temperature of the water. It should feel warm, but not hot. Pour the water and cooled melted butter into the flour mixture.

6. Sprinkle flour onto your work surface before kneading the dough for about 10 minutes. It should be smooth and elastic.

28

7. Brush a little oil inside a bowl and put the dough in it. Then brush the top of the dough with a little oil.

8. Cover the bowl with clear film and leave it in a warm place for 45 minutes. In the meantime, rub a baking sheet with a little oil to grease it.

9. Sprinkle your work surface with flour and knead the dough for a minute. Divide the dough into 12 pieces and roll each piece into a ball.

10. Put the balls on the baking sheet and cover them with a tea towel. Leave them in a warm place for 30 minutes. Preheat the oven to 200°C/400°F/Gas 6.

11. Brush the buns with milk, then bake them for 20 minutes, or until risen and golden.

12. Take the buns out of the oven. Lift them onto a wire rack to cool before serving.

Hot cross buns

On Good Friday — the Friday before Easter Sunday — Christians eat hot cross buns. The cross on top of these fruity buns reminds Christians of the cross on which Jesus died.

29

Pizza

This classic cheese and tomato pizza is called a Margarita. Once you have mastered this recipe, you can add different toppings such as spicy sausage, sweetcorn, peppers or tuna.

You will need

For 4 pizzas:
· 200g strong white bread flour, plus extra for dusting · 1 tsp easy-blend dried yeast · 1/2 tsp salt · 125ml warm water · 1 tbsp olive oil · 6 tbsp fresh tomato sauce · 100g grated mozzarella cheese · ground black pepper

Extra equipment

· sieve · clear film · rolling pin
· 2 baking sheets
Ask an adult to help you use the oven.

1. Sieve together the flour, yeast and salt. Make a well in the middle of the mixture.

2. Check the temperature of the water by putting your finger into it. It should feel just warm, but not hot.

3. Pour the water into the well and add the oil. Stir together to make a soft dough.

4. Sprinkle a little flour over your work surface, then put the dough on top. Sprinkle a little more flour on top of the dough, then knead it for about 10 minutes until it is smooth and elastic. If the dough is sticky, continue sprinkling on a little more flour as you work.

5. Wash your hands, then rub a little oil inside a clean bowl. Put the dough inside and pat your oily hands on the dough to make that oily, too. Cover the bowl with clear film and put it in a warm place for 1 hour until it has doubled in size.

30

6. About 15 minutes before the end of rising time, preheat the oven to 220°C/425°F/Gas 7.

7. Sprinkle a little flour onto the work surface and tip the dough on top. Press down on the dough to get rid of some of the air. Cut the dough into four equal pieces. Using a rolling pin, roll each piece into a 13 cm round.

8. Arrange the rounds on baking sheets. Spread about 1 1/2 tbsp of tomato sauce on top of each one and add a grinding of black pepper.

Pizza ovens

Traditionally pizzas were cooked in wood-fired brick ovens. The ovens were heated until they were very hot and the pizzas were put into the oven and taken out on a long wooden paddle. You can still see this in some pizza restaurants today.

9. Sprinkle cheese on top of each pizza. Put the baking sheets in the oven and bake for 12 minutes until the pizzas are golden and crisp on the edges.

10. Wearing oven gloves, take the baking sheets from the oven and place them on a heatproof surface. When the pizza is cool enough, cut it into slices and serve.

31

Tasty calzone

When you cut into this calzone, you will find a pizza filling inside the crispy crust. You can use all kinds of pizza fillings inside a calzone – this one has ham, ricotta cheese and tomato.

1. Sieve together the flour, yeast and salt. Make a well in the middle of the flour mixture.

2. Check the temperature of the water. It should feel just warm, but not hot.

3. Pour the water into the well and add the oil. Stir together to make a soft dough.

4. Sprinkle flour over your work surface, then knead the dough for about 10 minutes until it is smooth and elastic. If the dough is sticky, continue sprinkling on a little more flour as you knead.

5. Brush a little oil inside a clean bowl. Put the dough inside and brush a little oil on top of the dough. Cover with clear film and leave it to stand for 1 hour until the dough has doubled in size. After 45 minutes, preheat the oven to 220°C/425°C/Gas 7.

6. In the meantime, make the filling. Slice the tomatoes in half. Press your thumb into the seeds to remove them, then cut out the woody stem and throw it away. Roughly chop the flesh and put it in a bowl.

7. Add the ricotta and Parmesan to the tomatoes. Tear the ham into pieces and add them to the bowl. Tear the basil leaves into pieces and add them to the bowl, too. Add a grinding of black pepper and stir the mixture.

8. Sprinkle flour onto your work surface before pressing down on the dough to get rid of some of the air. Cut the dough into four pieces. Roll each piece into a 20-cm round.

9. Spoon a quarter of the filling onto half of each round, leaving a big border around the edge.

10. Fold over the top of the dough to make a half-moon shape. Press down around the outside and twist the edge of the dough to seal it. Put the calzone on a baking sheet, brush with a little oil and bake for 15 minutes until golden.

11. Wearing oven gloves, remove the baking sheet from the oven and put it on a heatproof surface. Lift each calzone onto a serving plate and serve.

34

Sandwiches and Snacks

Contents

All about sandwiches and snacks

Most sandwiches are made from two slices of bread with a filling spread in between. You can make all kinds of different sandwiches depending on your choice of bread and filling. Snacks are usually smaller than a meal and can be anything from a crunchy apple to potato wedges and a dip. Snacks should be easy to make and just enough to fill a gap.

Making a sandwich

Choosing the bread for your sandwich is important because the type of bread you choose will give the sandwich a particular taste and texture. Bread can be white, brown or wholemeal, or it can be made of rye, corn or other grains. Shaped breads, such as a French baguette or a bread roll, are good for turning into chunky sandwiches. Pitta breads can be split and the filling stuffed inside, while flatbreads, such as tortillas, can be rolled up around the filling to make a wrap. You can put all kinds of filling inside your sandwich. They can be sweet or savoury and you can add just one filling or you might decide to have several. Popular fillings include jam, cheese, ham, egg, tuna, chicken and hummus. You can also add salad, such as sliced cucumber and tomato, cress, lettuce and coleslaw. You might also want to add extra flavourings such as pickle, chutney or mayonnaise.

Simple snacks

Different types of snack are eaten all over the world. For example, if you lived in Italy, you may have some homemade bruschetta — tomato toasts — with some olives as an afternoon snack. If you lived in Mexico, nachos or quesadillas would be perfect to keep you going. Just like sandwiches, snacks can be sweet or savoury. Although snacks such as crisps, cakes and biscuits are delicious, they are not very healthy and should be eaten only as a treat. Instead, snack on fruit and vegetables, such as oranges, bananas and carrots.

Get started

In this chapter you can learn to make a whole range of sandwiches and snacks. All the recipes use everyday kitchen equipment, such as knives, spoons, forks and chopping boards. You can see pictures of some of the different equipment that you may need on pages 8—11. Before you start, check that you have all the equipment that you will need and make a list of any ingredients that you need to buy. Make sure there is an adult to help you, especially with the recipes that involve using the cooker or oven. When you have everything you need, make sure all the kitchen surfaces are clean and wash your hands well with soap and water. If you have long hair, tie it back. Always wash raw fruit and vegetables under cold running water before preparing or cooking them. This will help to remove any dirt and germs. Then, put on an apron and get cooking!

Creamy raita

This Indian dip is great for scooping up with poppadums. If you do not have poppadums, you could serve it with strips of red and orange peppers.

You will need

For 4 servings:
· 1/2 large cucumber
· 225ml Greek yogurt
· 1 garlic clove, peeled · 2 tbsp fresh mint
· pinch of salt · poppadums to serve

Extra equipment

· grater · sieve · garlic press

1. Cut the cucumber in half lengthways. Using a teaspoon, scrape out the seeds from each half and throw them away.

2. Grate each cucumber half. Be careful not to rub your fingers on the grater.

3. Put the cucumber in a sieve and hold it over the kitchen sink. Press down on the cucumber with your hand to squeeze out as much liquid as possible.

4. Tip the cucumber into a medium-sized bowl and add the yogurt.

5. Crush the garlic in a garlic press and add it to the cucumber and yogurt.

6. To chop the mint, pluck off the leaves from the stems until you have a small handful of leaves. Roll the leaves into a loose ball and gently rock a knife over the leaves. Do this until the leaves are finely chopped.

7. Add the mint and a pinch of salt to the yogurt and stir well. Taste the mixture and, if necessary, add a pinch more salt and stir.

8. Put the minty yogurt into a serving bowl and serve with the poppadums.

Minty cures

Mint not only adds flavour to food but it also has healing properties. Next time you have a tummy ache , put some mint leaves in hot water. Leave the water to cool, then sip the minty tea, it will help to settle your tummy ache.

Hummus wrap

A wrap is a kind of sandwich, but instead of putting the filling between two slices of bread, you roll it up inside a single flatbread. You can put all kinds of sandwich filling inside a wrap. When you have mastered this one, why not try another filling?

You will need
For 1 serving:
- 1/4 red pepper
- 1 tortilla wrap
- 2 tbsp hummus
- handful of salad leaves

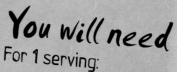

1. Put the pepper on the chopping board and gently pull out any seeds and leftover pith. Cut the pepper into small pieces and set them aside for later.

2. Put the tortilla on a board and spread the hummus over it.

Delicious hummus

To make your own hummus, rinse and drain a tin of chickpeas. Blend them together with 1 crushed clove of garlic, 1 teaspoon of ground cumin, 1 teaspoon of ground coriander, 4 tablespoons of olive oil, 2 tablespoons of lemon juice and 1 tablespoon of tahini (sesame seed paste).

3. Sprinkle the chopped pepper over one half of the tortilla.

4. Scatter the salad leaves on top of the chopped pepper.

5. To roll up the tortilla, start rolling from the edge of the half that has the salad and peppers. Tuck in any stray leaves as you roll. The half of the wrap that is covered with hummus but has no chopped pepper or salad leaves will help to stick the wrap together.

6. Cut the wrap in half across the middle to make two smaller wraps. Put them on a plate and serve.

Classic egg mayo

If you like this classic recipe, try putting a few slices of cucumber or tomato on top of the egg mixture or adding a sprinkling of cress. You could try using different types of bread, such as rye or a baguette, too.

You will need

For 1 serving:
· 1 egg · water · 1 tbsp mayonnaise
· salt and black pepper · 2 slices wholegrain bread

Extra equipment

· Slotted spoon
Ask an adult to help you use the cooker.

(1.) Put the egg in a small saucepan and pour cold water over the top to cover the egg by about 3cm.

(2.) Bring the water to the boil — when you see bubbles, the water is boiling. Turn down the heat and let the water simmer gently for 10 minutes.

(3.) Turn off the heat and take the egg out of the water using a slotted spoon. Put the egg in a bowl of cold water and leave it to cool.

Fresh eggs

As an egg gets older, the white and yolk start to change. If you compared a very fresh egg with a ten-day old egg and a 20-day old egg you would see a big difference. The very fresh egg would have a fat, rounded yolk and two layers of white. As an egg gets older, the yolk becomes flatter and the difference between the two layers of white becomes less and less until you can hardly notice it at all.

4. When the egg is cool, tap it against your work surface until the shell is cracked all over. Peel off the shell and rinse the egg under cold water to remove any leftover bits of shell.

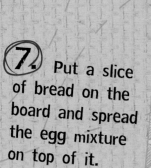

5. Cut the egg into small pieces and put it in a clean bowl.

6. Add the mayonnaise, a pinch of salt and a grinding of black pepper to the egg and stir to mix.

7. Put a slice of bread on the board and spread the egg mixture on top of it.

8. Place the second slice of bread on top and press down gently to make sure it is secure. Cut your sandwich in half from corner to corner to serve.

45

Bruschetta

You will need
For 4 servings:
· 2 tomatoes · salt and pepper · 1 1/4 tsp olive oil · 1 small baguette · 1 garlic clove
· 8 fresh basil leaves

Extra equipment
Ask an adult to help you use the cooker.

Open sandwiches are ones that do not have a second slice of bread on top. Bruschetta are little Italian toasts that come somewhere between a mini open sandwich and a snack.

1. Cut each tomato in half. Using your thumb, gently press out the seeds and jelly and throw them away.

2. Finely chop the tomatoes and put them in a bowl. Sprinkle a pinch of salt and a grinding of black pepper over the tomatoes. Then pour over 1 teaspoon of the olive oil and stir the mixture gently. Set aside for later.

3. Wipe and dry the chopping board. Cut off the end of the baguette, then cut eight slices, about 1.5cm thick.

4. Turn on the grill. If it is an electric grill, leave it to heat up for about 5 minutes. Arrange the bread slices on the grill rack and toast them so that both sides are golden.

5. Arrange the toasts on a serving plate. Cut the garlic clove in half and rub the cut side over the top of each slice of toast. Garlic has a very strong taste, so you only need to rub the toasts gently to give them a good garlicky flavour.

6. Spoon the chopped tomatoes and any juices from the bowl on top of the toasts. Drizzle the rest of the olive oil over each of the toasts.

7. Top each of the toasts with a basil leaf before you serve the bruschetta.

Antipasti

In Italy, little snacks such as bruschetta, olives, marinated vegetables and cold meats are served as an appetizer before the main meal. These little snacks are called antipasti, which means 'before the meal'.

Quesadilla wedges

Quesadillas are a kind of fried sandwich from Mexico. This quesadilla is made with plain cheese, but in Mexico chillies; vegetables, such as spinach or peppers; and ham are used in quesadillas.

You will need
For 4 servings:
· 60g Cheddar cheese · 2 plain tortillas
· ground black pepper · tomato salsa

Extra equipment
· Grater · frying pan · spatula
Ask an adult to help you use the cooker.

1. Grate the cheese onto a small plate. Be careful not to grate your fingers!

2. Heat a large non-stick frying pan over a medium heat.

3. Put a tortilla in the pan. Sprinkle the cheese over the tortilla in an even layer and grind over some black pepper.

Grate away

The easiest way to grate cheese is to use a box-shaped cheese grater. Hold the grater firmly in one hand on a plate or board. Hold the block of cheese in the other hand and hold it against the top of the grater. Slide the cheese down against the teeth of the grater and shreds of cheese will fall down inside the grater. Continue in the same way until you have grated enough cheese for your recipe.

4. Put the second tortilla on top of the cheese and cook for about 3 minutes until the bottom tortilla is crisp and golden underneath. Check by lifting up the edge of the tortilla with a spatula.

5. Slide the spatula under the tortilla and carefully flip over the whole quesadilla.

6. Cook for a further 2 minutes until the quesadilla is golden on the second side.

7. Carefully slide the quesadilla onto a large chopping board and cut it in half. Cut it in half again so that you have four quarters. Then cut each quarter in half to make eight wedges.

8. Pile the quesadilla wedges onto a plate and serve them straightaway, on their own or with some tomato salsa for dipping.

Chunky wedges and dip

These potato wedges make a really filling snack or a lunchtime treat. Be careful when you eat them as they will be piping hot when you take them out of the oven!

You will need
For 4 servings:
- 1 large potato, scrubbed and patted dry
- 1 tbsp olive oil · salt and ground black pepper · 100ml natural yogurt
- 2 tsp pesto

Extra equipment
· baking sheet · pastry brush
Ask an adult to help you use the oven

1. Preheat the oven to 190°C/375°F/Gas 5.

2. Cut the potato in half. Place the two halves on their flat sides and cut them into quarters. Cut each quarter into chunky wedges — like big chips.

3. Put the potato wedges on a baking sheet in a single layer. Brush on the olive oil, sprinkle over a pinch of salt and grind over some black pepper. Toss to coat the wedges so that they are glossy all over.

Potatoes

Today, potatoes are eaten all over the world. However, this was not always the case. The very first potatoes were grown in South America and there is evidence that they were eaten in Peru as far back as 2,000 years ago. Europeans first tasted potatoes in 1537 in what is now Colombia.

4. Bake the wedges for about 20 minutes. Wearing oven gloves, take the baking sheet out of the oven and put it on a heatproof surface. Use a spatula to turn over the wedges. Put the baking sheet back in the oven, and bake the wedges for another 15 minutes until they are golden all over and tender.

5. Meanwhile, stir together the yogurt and pesto and spoon the mixture into a serving bowl.

6. When the potatoes are golden, wearing oven gloves, remove the baking sheet from the oven and lift the wedges onto a serving dish. Serve hot with the dip.

Chicken pitta pocket

You will need

For 1 serving:
· 1 carrot · 1/2 a grilled chicken breast, about 75g · 1/2 tsp sweet chilli sauce · 1 tsp olive oil · 1/2 tsp white wine vinegar · salt · 1 pitta bread · small handful of salad leaves

Extra equipment

· Vegetable peeler · grater
Ask an adult to help you to use the grill

You can buy ready-grilled chicken breasts for this recipe – or you can ask an adult to grill a chicken breast for you. You could also use leftover cold roast chicken.

1. Cut off each end of the carrot. Using a vegetable peeler, peel off the skin.

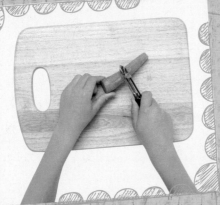

2. Grate the carrot and put the grated pieces in a medium-sized bowl.

3. Put the chicken on the board and cut it into bite-sized pieces. Add it to the grated carrot.

4. To make the dressing, put the sweet chilli sauce, olive oil and vinegar into a small bowl. Add a pinch of salt and stir the mixture well.

5. Pour the dressing over the carrots and chicken and mix it well.

6. Turn on the grill. If you are using an electric grill, leave it for about 5 minutes to heat up. Put the pitta bread under the grill and warm it for a few minutes on each side until it starts to puff up.

7. Put the bread on the board — it will be full of hot steam that can burn, so be careful! Cut the bread in half and carefully open up the halves to make two pockets.

8. Put a couple of salad leaves in each pitta pocket, then spoon the chicken and carrot salad on top. Eat warm or cold.

Pitta bread

This soft, chewy flatbread is eaten all over the Middle East. It is made of wheat and is slightly leavened. When it is baked, the oval-shaped bread puffs up, leaving it hollow inside. This hollow makes a kind of pocket that makes pitta bread perfect for stuffing to make a kind of sandwich.

Tuna melt

This is a classic open sandwich topped with tuna mayonnaise and melting cheese. Adding chopped cornichon or dill pickle to the tuna mixture adds a tangy bite, but if you prefer to leave it out, the tuna also tastes great on ts own.

You will need

For 2 servings:
- 200g can tuna, drained
- 2 cornichons or 1 large dill pickle (optional) · 3 tbsp mayonnaise
- freshly ground black pepper
- 2 thick slices bread
- 2 large slices Jarlsberg or Swiss cheese, such as Emmental

Extra equipment

Ask an adult to help you use the grill.

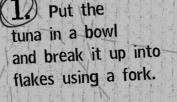

1. Put the tuna in a bowl and break it up into flakes using a fork.

2. If using cornichons or dill pickle, put them on a board and chop finely. Add them to the tuna.

3. Add the mayonnaise and a grinding of black pepper to the tuna. Mix everything together.

4. Turn on the grill. If you are using an electric grill, leave it for about 5 minutes to heat up. Arrange the bread slices on the grill pan and place them under the grill for a few minutes to toast one side.

Both Jarlsberg and Emmental cheese are made in similar ways and have the same kind of mild flavour. They are both full of holes, too. The holes appear when the cheese is made. Several bacteria are used to make the cheeses and while the cheeses mature, the bacteria produce carbon dioxide. This gas forms big bubbles in the cheese, which makes the holes.

5. Spread the untoasted side of bread with the tuna mixture.

6. Top each slice of toast with a slice of cheese and then place the toast under the grill until the cheese bubbles.

7. Carefully slide the toasts onto plates. You could serve the toast with a side salad of coleslaw.

55

56

Vegetarian Food

Contents

All about vegetarian food

A vegetarian is someone who does not eat meat, fish or animal products such as gelatine, which is made from animal bones. There are many reasons why people choose to be vegetarian. For some people, their religion does not allow them to eat meat. Other people feel it is wrong to eat meat. Some people just prefer to eat other things instead.

Eating protein

If you decide not to eat meat or fish, it is very important that you still eat protein. Protein helps you to grow and helps your body to repair itself. Meat and fish provide protein. If you cut them out of your diet, you must replace them with other protein foods. Good sources of vegetarian protein include cheese, nuts, tofu, quorn, beans and other pulses, such as chickpeas.

A balanced diet

As well as eating protein-rich foods, you must eat other types of food to have a balanced diet. These include carbohydrates, dairy products, fruit and vegetables. Carbohydrates are starchy foods such as potatoes, pasta, rice and bread. These foods give you energy. Cheese and yogurt are dairy products that contain calcium, which is important for strong bones and teeth. Fruit and vegetables contain vitamins and nutrients, which are important for maintaining a healthy body. Carbohydrates should make up about one-third of what you eat every day. Fruit and vegetables should make up about one-third, too. The rest of your food should be protein, such as nuts, and dairy, such as cheese. You can eat some foods containing fat and sugar, but these foods are less good for you so it is best not to eat too many of them.

Get started

In this chapter you can learn to make all kinds of vegetarian food. All the recipes use everyday kitchen equipment, such as knives, spoons, forks and chopping boards. You can see pictures of the different equipment that you may need on page 8–11. Before you start, check that you have all the equipment that you will need and make a list of any ingredients that you need to buy. Make sure there is an adult to help you, especially with the recipes that involve using the cooker or oven. When you have everything you need, make sure all the kitchen surfaces are clean and wash your hands well with soap and water. If you have long hair, tie it back. Always wash raw fruit and vegetables under cold running water before preparing or cooking them. This will help to remove any dirt and germs. Then, put on an apron and get cooking!

Tasty hummus

This creamy dip is packed with protein and makes a great snack. If you don't have a food processor or a hand-held blender, you can use a potato masher instead. Simply put all the ingredients in a bowl and mash until smooth.

You will need
For 4 servings:
· 400g can chickpeas, rinsed · 1 garlic clove, peeled · 1 tsp ground cumin · 1 tsp ground coriander · 4 tbsp olive oil · 1 tbsp tahini · 2 tbsp lemon juice · salt and ground black pepper · 3 carrots, peeled · 2 pitta breads

Extra equipment
· food processor or hand-held blender
· toaster

1. Put the chickpeas in a food processor. If you have a hand-held blender, put them in a large bowl.

2. Slice the garlic finely and add it to the chickpeas.

3. Add the cumin, coriander, olive oil, tahini and lemon juice to the chickpeas. Add a pinch of salt and a grinding of black pepper.

4. Blend all the ingredients together until the mixture is smooth. If necessary, turn off the food processor or blender part of the way through, scrape down the sides of the bowl or food processor using a spatula, then blend again.

5. Taste the hummus and add more salt and black pepper if necessary. If the hummus is very thick, add a teaspoon of water and blend again until smooth. Spoon the hummus into a serving bowl.

6. Cut off the ends of each carrot. Cut the carrots in half lengthways then lay the halves on their flat sides and cut into sticks. Put the carrot sticks into another serving dish.

7. Toast the pitta breads until they are golden. When they are cool, cut them into fingers.

8. Put the pitta fingers in a dish and serve with the hummus and carrot sticks.

Tahini

Tahini is a creamy paste made of ground sesame seeds that is used in Middle Eastern dips. It has a savoury, nutty taste and helps to give hummus its distinctive flavour.

Tricolore salad

This is a traditional salad that you will find on the menu in Italian restaurants. Tricolore, which is pronounced 'tree-co-lor-ay', means three colours. The name reflects the three colours of the salad: red tomato, green avocado and white mozzarella. These are also the colours of the Italian flag.

You will need
For 4 servings:
· 2 tomatoes · 1 ball of mozzarella (about 150g) · 1 avocado
· 2 tsp red wine vinegar · small pinch of sugar · 5 tsp extra virgin olive oil
· salt and black pepper

1. Put four plates on your work surface. Cut the tomatoes into slices about 6mm thick. Arrange a quarter of the slices on each serving plate.

2. Cut the mozzarella ball in half and then cut each half into slices about 6mm thick. Arrange a quarter of the slices on each plate with the tomatoes.

3. Cut into the avocado lengthways, all the way down to the stone, then all the way round the stone. Holding half of the avocado in each hand, twist the halves in opposite directions so that they come apart.

Keeping them green!

When some fruits, such as apples and avocados, are cut, their flesh turns brown because it reacts with the oxygen in air. It does not make the fruit harmful to eat but it does not look nice. This is why you should serve this salad as soon as you have made it.

4. Ask an adult to help you remove the stone from the avocado.

5. Cut each avocado half in half again and peel off the skin. Cut the avocado into slices about 6mm thick. Arrange a quarter of the slices on each plate with the tomato and mozzarella.

6. To make the dressing, whisk the vinegar, sugar and olive oil together and season it with a pinch of salt and a grinding of black pepper. Drizzle the dressing over the salads and serve straight away.

Scrambled eggs

Eggs are a good source of protein. You can eat scrambled eggs for breakfast, lunch or dinner, but if you want to serve them as a main meal, you should have them with vegetables or a side salad.

You will need

For 1 serving:
- 2 eggs · salt and black pepper
- 2 slices bread · a knob of butter, plus extra for spreading on the toast

Extra equipment
· toaster
Ask an adult to help you use the cooker.

1. Crack the eggs into a bowl and mix them up with a fork.

2. Put the bread in a toaster to toast.

How to crack an egg

1. Hold the egg in one hand and knock the middle on the side of a bowl to make a deep crack in its shell.
2. Holding the egg over the bowl, put your thumbs into the crack.
3. Pull the halves apart so that the egg falls into the bowl. Check that no bits of shell have fallen into the bowl.

1

2

3

3. Put a non-stick pan over a medium heat and melt the knob of butter. When the butter sizzles, pour in the eggs. Stir the eggs with a wooden spatula, scraping it across the bottom of the pan to break up the egg as it sets.

4. When the eggs are set but still moist, take the pan off the heat. The eggs will continue cooking, so it is important that they are still moist and not completely cooked when you take the pan off the heat.

5. When the toast is ready, put it on a plate and spread it with butter.

6. Give the eggs a stir, then spoon them onto the toast. Grind over a little more black pepper and they are ready to eat.

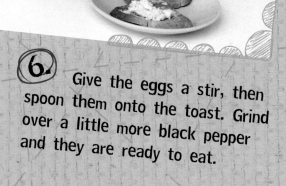

Tofu kebabs

These healthy skewers make a tasty lunch or supper dish. Once you have mastered this recipe, you could try using courgettes and orange peppers instead of the tomatoes and yellow pepper.

You will need
For 4 servings:
- 1 yellow pepper · 1 red onion, peeled
- 300g firm tofu · 150g cherry tomatoes
- 2 tbsp hoi sin sauce · 1 tsp soy sauce
- 2 tsp sunflower oil · 1 tsp lime juice

Extra equipment
- 8 wooden skewers · kitchen towel
- aluminium foil · pastry brush

Ask an adult to help you use the grill.

1. Soak the skewers in water while you make the rest of the recipe. This will stop the sticks from burning when they are under the grill.

2. Cut the pepper in half lengthways through the green stalk. Pull the two halves apart, then cut around the stalk and throw it away. Pull out the seeds and white pith and throw that away, too. Cut each half into quarters and then into chunks. Set aside the chunks for later.

3. Place the onion upright on the board and cut it in half. Put each half on its flat side and cut each one into quarters. Divide each quarter into layers and set them aside to use later.

4. Cut the tofu into 2 cm cubes. Set them aside for later.

5. Dry the skewers on a clean kitchen towel.

6. Thread layers of pepper, onion, tofu and tomato onto the skewers.

7. To make the marinade, put the hoi sin sauce, soy sauce, sunflower oil and lime juice in a small bowl and mix them together.

8. Turn on the grill. If you are using an electric grill, leave it to heat up for about 5 minutes. In the meantime, line the grill pan with aluminium foil and arrange the skewers on top.

9. Brush about half the marinade onto the skewers and grill them for about 5 minutes. Turn the skewers over and brush them with more marinade. Grill for another 3 minutes until they are golden and ready to eat. Why not try them with some rice or pasta salad?

Tofu

Tofu is made from soya beans. The beans are soaked in water, then ground and boiled with water. This mixture is strained to make a white liquid. Things are added to the liquid so that it 'sticks together' to become more solid — a bit like cheese. The cheese-like mixture is then pressed to squeeze out the liquid. The end result is firm, white tofu.

69

Couscous salad

Couscous is a carbohydrate made from wheat. It looks like a grain and has a slightly nutty flavour. The butter beans in this salad are packed with protein and the peppers and tomatoes are full of vitamins and minerals.

1. Cut the pepper in half lengthways through the green stalk. Pull the two halves apart, then cut around the stalk and throw it away. Pull out the seeds and white pith and throw them away. Cut the flesh into bite-sized pieces, about 2 cm square, and put them into a small bowl.

2. Cut each tomato in half and add them to the peppers.

In the wash

It is important to wash vegetables and fruit before you eat or cook them. Fruit and vegetables grown with the help of fertilisers and pesticides may still have chemicals on them, which could harm your body. Organic fruit and vegetables will not have chemicals on them but they may be dirty, so wash them, too.

3. Pull the basil leaves from the stalks and throw the stalks away. Gently tear the leaves into little pieces and add them to the bowl with the tomatoes and peppers.

4. Boil the water in a kettle. Put the couscous in a large bowl and sprinkle over a pinch of salt. When the water has boiled, pour it over the couscous.

5. Leave the couscous to stand for 5 minutes until it has soaked up all the water. Run a fork through it to separate the grains.

6. To make the dressing, put the lemon juice, olive oil and honey in a bowl and add a pinch of salt and a grinding of black pepper. Whisk it all together until it is mixed.

7. Add the beans, peppers, tomatoes and basil to the couscous and pour over the dressing.

8. Using two large spoons, fold the ingredients together. Start with the spoons at the bottom of the bowl and slowly bring them to the top, stirring the ingredients together as you go. When the salad is well mixed, spoon it into four bowls to serve.

71

Minestrone soup

Minestrone is a classic Italian pasta soup. This recipe suggests using vermicelli pasta but you can use other pasta shapes that are made especially for soups.

You will need

For 4 servings:
· 1 onion, peeled · 2 garlic cloves · 2 tbsp olive oil · 400g can chopped tomatoes
· 1 tbsp sun-dried tomato puree
· 1.2 litres vegetable stock
· 1 carrot · 115g green beans
· 60g vermicelli · ground black pepper

Extra equipment

· Peeler
Ask an adult to help you use the cooker.

1. Cut the onion in half and then chop each half finely. Set aside for later.

2. Peel the garlic cloves. Put each clove in a garlic press to crush it.

3. Heat the oil in a saucepan over a medium heat. Add the onion and garlic and fry for 4 minutes.

Watery eyes

Onions contain natural chemicals called allicins. When you cut up onions, you release these chemicals and when the allicins react with your eyes, they can make them sting and water.

4. Add the tomatoes, tomato puree and stock. Bring to the boil, then turn the heat to low and cover the saucepan with a lid. Simmer for 15 minutes.

5. While the soup simmers, peel the carrot. Cut off both ends, then cut the carrot in half lengthways and in half again. Slice the quartered carrots thinly and set them aside to use later.

6. Cut off the very end of each bean and then slice each bean into 1cm lengths. Set aside to use later.

7. When the soup has been simmering for 15 minutes, carefully take off the lid and add the carrots and beans. Put the lid back on and let the soup simmer for a further 5 minutes.

8. Add the pasta and simmer for 2 minutes more until the pasta is tender. Season with black pepper, then ladle the soup into bowls to serve.

73

Jacket potato with chilli beans

You can make the chilli beans as spicy hot as you like. If you like things extra hot, add a pinch more chilli, or if you do not like things hot at all, leave out the chilli and add black pepper instead.

You will need

For 4 servings:
· 4 baking potatoes · oil for step 1
· 1 onion · 1 garlic clove, peeled · 2 tbsp olive oil · 400g can kidney beans, rinsed and drained · 400g can chopped tomatoes
· 1 tbsp tomato puree · 1 tsp ground cumin
· 1/8 tsp crushed dried chilli · butter · plain yogurt

Extra equipment

· Garlic press
Ask an adult to help you use the oven.

1. Preheat the oven to 190°C/375°F/Gas 5. Prick the potatoes all over. Rub a little oil over each potato and sprinkle with salt.

2. Bake the potatoes for about 1 hour until they are crisp on the outside and soft in the middle. To test whether a potato is cooked, put a knife into the potato. It should feel soft all the way through.

3. While the potatoes bake, make the chilli. Put the onion on a chopping board and slice off both ends. Slit the brown skin and peel it off, then chop the onion finely.

4. Use a garlic press to crush the garlic.

74

5. Heat the olive oil in a pan over a medium heat. Fry the onion and garlic for 5 minutes.

6. Add the beans, tomatoes, tomato puree, cumin and chilli to the saucepan. Let the mixture boil, then reduce the heat to low and cover the saucepan with a lid. Simmer for 25 minutes, stirring occasionally, then turn off the heat.

7. When the potatoes are cooked, warm through the chilli again if it is not hot enough.

8. Wearing oven gloves, put each potato on a plate. Cut a deep cross in the top of each potato to open it.

9. Add a knob of butter to each potato, then top with some chilli and plain yogurt.

Potato tubers

If farmers left potatoes underground, roots and stems would grow from them into a new plant. The part of the potato plant that we eat is called a tuber.

Chunky pasta

Timing is important when you cook pasta dishes. You should aim for the pasta and sauce to be ready at the same time so that everything is perfectly cooked.

You will need

For 4 servings:
· 150g mushrooms · 1 large courgette
· 2 garlic cloves, peeled · 2 tbsp olive oil
· 400g can chopped tomatoes · 1/4 tsp dried oregano · salt and ground black pepper · 300g dried penne or other pasta shapes · grated cheese

Extra equipment
· Garlic press · colander
Ask an adult to help you use the cooker.

1. Cut the mushrooms into slices about 6mm thick and set them aside for later.

2. Put the courgette onto a board and cut off both ends. Slice the courgette in half lengthways and then place each half on the board, cut side down. Cut each half lengthways into three long strips. Cut each strip into chunks. Set them aside.

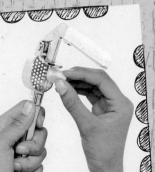

3. Crush each garlic clove in a garlic press.

4. To make the sauce, heat the oil over a medium heat. Add the garlic and fry it for about 1 minute — be careful not to let it burn.

5. Add the mushrooms and fry gently for 5 minutes, stirring occasionally. Add the tomatoes and oregano and season the mixture with a pinch of salt and black pepper. Bring the sauce to the boil, then turn the heat to low. Simmer the sauce for 10 minutes.

6. Add the courgettes and a pinch more salt. Stir the sauce then let it simmer for about 15 minutes, stirring occasionally, until the courgettes are tender but not completely soft.

7. While the courgettes cook, cook the pasta by following the instructions on the packet. When the pasta is cooked, drain it and add it to the sauce. Mix it all together and spoon it into serving bowls. Spinkle on some grated cheese before you serve the pasta.

Pasta

There are hundreds of different types of pasta. Long pasta includes spaghetti and vermicelli; short pasta includes penne. Ravioli is a popular stuffed pasta and lasagne is a flat pasta that is baked in the oven.

78

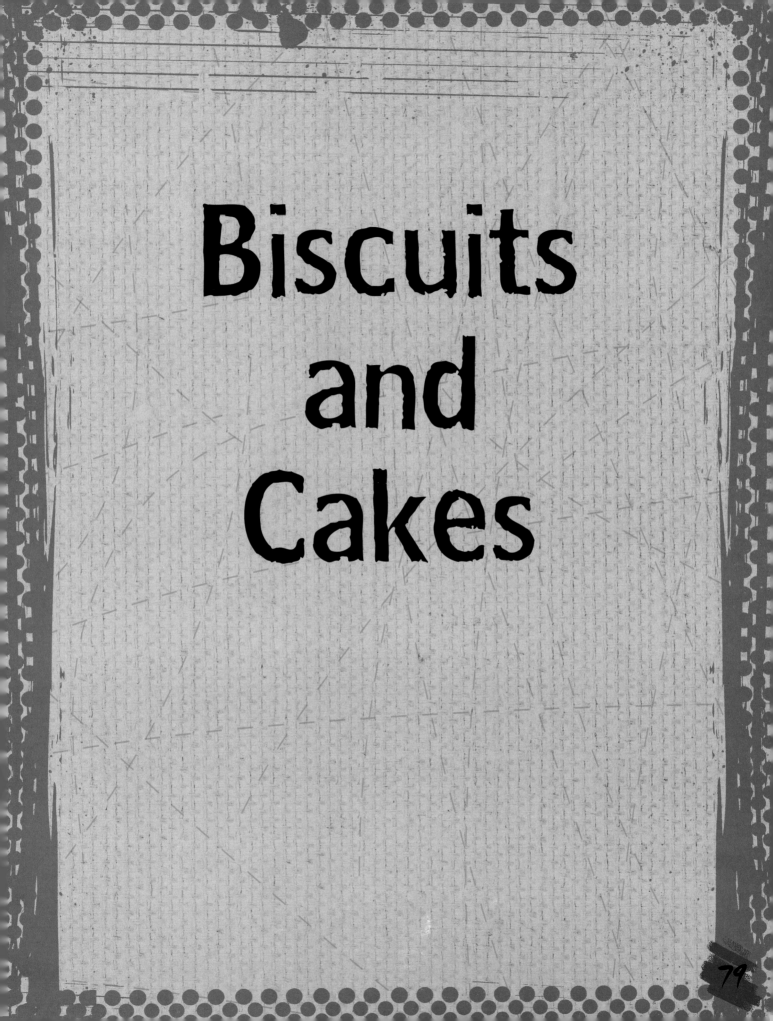

Biscuits and Cakes

Contents

All about biscuits and cakes

There are many kinds of biscuit and cake. They can have different tastes, textures, colours and shapes depending on the ingredients used. Often they are sweet, but they can be savoury, too. Most biscuits and cakes are baked in the oven, but some do not need baking and are chilled in the fridge instead.

Different kinds of biscuits and cakes

Butter, sugar, eggs and flour are the main ingredients used to make biscuits and cakes. But you can add other ingredients such as oats, syrup, dried fruit, chocolate and nuts. The way you combine and cook these ingredients can give miraculous results. Different combinations will produce different kinds of biscuit and cake. Some will be soft and chewy, some will be crisp and crumbly, while others will be light and airy.

Baking sheets and tins

Cakes and biscuits are usually baked in some kind of tin or case. For example, little cupcake cases can be used to make fairy cakes or if you are making a large cake, you would use sandwich cake tins, which are perfect for stacking one cake on top of another. Biscuits and cookies are often cooked on baking sheets, these are metal trays that can go in the oven.

Different decorations

Most biscuits and cakes can be served plain – but they can be decorated, too. This not only looks pretty and tastes good, but it can also be great fun! You can decorate cakes and cookies before baking. Try sprinkling flaked nuts or coarse sugar on top of cakes or soft cookie mixtures. Alternatively, you can press on whole nuts or glacé fruits. Some people prefer to decorate cakes and cookies once they have been baked. Simple glacé icing or butter icing is easy to make (see page 98–99) and can be spooned or spread on top of a cooked cake or biscuit. If you like, you can add more decorations. Pretty coloured sweets, hundreds and thousands or fruit and nuts all look good. You could also add a dusting of icing sugar to cakes.

Get started

In this chapter you can learn to make all kinds of biscuits and cakes. All the recipes use everyday kitchen equipment, such as knives, spoons, forks and chopping boards. You can see pictures of the different equipment that you may need on pages 8–11. Before you start, check that you have all the equipment that you will need and make a list of any ingredients you need to buy. Check too that there is an adult to help you, especially with the recipes that involve using the cooker or oven. When you have everything you need, make sure all the kitchen surfaces are clean and wash your hands well with soap and water. If you have long hair, tie it back.

Fruity flapjacks

These chewy flapjacks make a great treat to pop into your lunchbox. The flapjacks will look soft when you take them out of the oven, but they firm up when they cool.

You will need
For 16 flapjacks:
- 125g butter, plus extra for greasing
- 75g ready-to-eat dried apricots
- 125g demerara sugar · 5 tbsp golden syrup · 200g rolled oats
- 2 tbsp sunflower seeds
- 2 tbsp pumpkin seeds

Extra equipment
· 20cm x 20cm cake tin
Ask an adult to help you use the cooker and oven.

1. Preheat the oven to 180°C/350°F/Gas 4. Grease the cake tin with butter, making sure the base and sides are coated all over.

2. Roughly chop the apricots and set them aside for later.

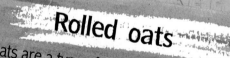

3. Put the butter, sugar and syrup in a pan and set it over a very low heat. Stir now and then, until the butter has melted.

Rolled oats
Oats are a type of cereal that grow well in moist, cool climates. The grains are steamed and flattened to make rolled oats. In many countries, rolled oats are eaten as a breakfast porridge or mixed with fruit and seeds to make muesli or cereal.

4. When the butter has melted, remove the pan from the heat and stir the mixture well. Add the oats, seeds and apricots and stir again.

5. Pour the mixture into the tin and spread it out in an even layer. Make sure you push the mixture right into the corners of the tin.

6. Bake for about 25 minutes until golden. Wearing a pair of oven gloves, take the tin out of the oven and put it on a heatproof surface.

7. Leave the flapjack to cool in the tin. When cool, cut it into quarters. Then cut each quarter into four squares to make 16 squares in total.

Chocolate chip cookies

These simple biscuits, made with a creamed butter and sugar mixture, are a classic cookie. The soft mixture needs no shaping and can simply be dropped onto baking sheets in big dollops.

1. Preheat the oven to 190°C/375°F/ Gas 5. Grease the baking sheets with butter.

2. Put the butter and sugar in a bowl and beat them together with a wooden spoon until they make a smooth, creamy mixture.

4. Put the flour and baking powder in a clean bowl and mix them together. Sieve the flour into the butter mixture and stir until the mixture is creamy and well blended.

You will need
For 20 cookies:
- 115g butter at room temperature, plus extra for greasing
- 85g caster sugar · 1 egg, lightly beaten
- 1 tsp vanilla essence · 150g plain flour
- 1/2 tsp baking powder
- 100g chocolate chips

Extra equipment
· 3 baking sheets · sieve · wire rack
Ask an adult to help you use the oven.

3. Gradually add the egg to the butter mixture and beat well. Add the vanilla essence and beat the mixture until everything is mixed together.

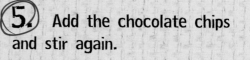

5. Add the chocolate chips and stir again.

Use a teaspoon to scoop up heaped spoonfuls of the mixture. Using another teaspoon, scrape the mixture onto the baking sheets. Space the blobs of cookie mixture well apart to allow them to spread during cooking. You should end up with about eight blobs of mixture on each baking sheet.

7. Bake the cookies for about 8 minutes until they are golden.

8. Using a pair of oven gloves, take the baking sheets out of the oven and put them on a heatproof surface. Leave the cookies to firm up for about 1 minute. When firm, lift the cookies onto a wire rack to cool.

Making cakes and biscuits rise

Baking powder is a raising agent used to make cakes and biscuits rise. It is made from an alkali ingredient (bicarbonate of soda) and an acidic ingredient (cream of tartar). When these two ingredients come into contact with a wet ingredient, they react to make carbon dioxide. The carbon dioxide makes tiny bubbles in the cake or biscuit mixture, which cause it to rise.

Cheesy biscuits

These savoury biscuits are flavoured with tangy Cheddar cheese. When you want a treat, they make a great alternative to a traditional sweet biscuit.

You will need
For 15 biscuits:
· 115g butter, at room temperature, plus extra for greasing · 115g Cheddar cheese · black pepper · 150g self-raising flour · cold water

Extra equipment
· 2 baking sheets · sieve · wire rack
Ask an adult to help you use the oven.

1. Preheat the oven to 180°C/350°F/ Gas 4. Grease two baking sheets with butter, making sure the surface is coated all over.

2. Grate the cheese.

3. Put the butter and cheese in a bowl and add a good grinding of black pepper. Beat them together until they make a soft, creamy mixture.

4. Sieve the flour into the butter mixture. Stir the mixture together and then bring it together with your hands.

5. Break off walnut-sized lumps of mixture and roll them between your hands to make round balls. Place them on the baking sheets, spacing them well apart.

6. Dip a fork into cold water, then gently press onto the top of each ball to flatten it. You will need to keep dipping the fork in water to stop it sticking to the biscuit mixture.

7. Bake the biscuits for 15-20 minutes until they are golden brown.

8. Using a pair of oven gloves, take the baking sheets out of the oven and put them on a heatproof surface. Leave the biscuits to cool for a minute then use a metal spatula to lift them onto a wire rack to cool.

Cooling cookies

Most cookies need to be moved to a wire rack to cool soon after baking. This allows cool air to circulate all around the cookie, making sure it stays crisp. If the cookie was left on the baking sheet, condensation (or moisture) would make it soggy.

Victoria sandwich cake

This cake is made using a classic cake mixture. It uses equal weights of butter, sugar, eggs and flour. It is one of the easiest and most tasty sandwich cakes to make.

You will need
For 1 sandwich cake:
· 175g butter, at room temperature, plus extra for greasing · 175g caster sugar · 3 eggs · 175g self-raising flour · 4 tbsp strawberry jam · 1 tbsp icing sugar

Extra equipment
· Greaseproof paper · 2x20cm sandwich tins · pencil · scissors · sieve · 2 wire racks
Ask an adult to help you use the oven.

1. Preheat the oven to 180°C/350°F/Gas 4.

2. Cut off enough greaseproof paper to cover both sandwich tins. Place one of the tins on the edge of the paper and draw around it to make a circle. Repeat to make a second circle. Cut out the circles and check that they fit inside the tins. Set them aside.

3. Grease the inside of each tin with butter then slip a paper circle into the base of each tin and press it down flat.

4. Put the butter and sugar in a bowl and beat them until they are smooth and creamy. Break one egg into the mixture and beat the mixture well. Beat in another egg, then add the last egg and beat the mixture again.

5. Sieve the flour over the butter mixture then stir it gently until the mixture is creamy.

6. Spoon half of the mixture into one tin and spread it out with the back of the spoon. Spoon the remaining mixture into the second tin and spread it out.

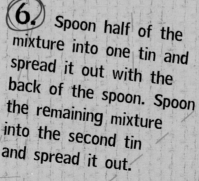

How to crack an egg

1. Hold the egg in one hand and knock the middle on the side of a bowl to make a deep crack in its shell.

2. Holding the egg over the bowl, put your thumbs into the crack.

3. Pull the halves apart so that the egg falls into the bowl. Check that no bits of shell have fallen into the bowl.

7. Bake for 20–25 minutes until each cake is golden and risen. To test if the cake is cooked, poke a skewer into the centre – it should come out clean. If the mixture sticks to the skewer then put the cake back into the oven for a few minutes more.

8. Use oven gloves to take the cakes out of the oven and put them on a heatproof surface. Ask an adult to help you to transfer the cakes to wire racks. Peel off the greaseproof paper and leave the cakes to cool.

9. when cool, put one cake the right way up on a plate. Ask an adult to help you slice a thin layer off the top of the cake to give it a flat surface. Spread the top with jam, then place the second cake on top.

10. Put the icing sugar in a sieve and hold it over the cake. Tap the side until the top of the cake is dusted with a layer of icing sugar.

Banana and fig muffins

Muffins are great for a weekend breakfast or brunch, or a teatime treat with a glass of milk. They are best eaten on the day you make them – that is why this recipe makes only six at a time.

You will need
For 6 muffins:
· 50g butter · 125g self-raising flour
· 1/2 tsp baking powder · 1/4 tsp bicarbonate of soda · 60g caster sugar
· 1 large ripe banana, peeled · 1 egg
· 50ml milk · 4 ready-to-eat dried figs

Extra equipment
· 6-hole muffin tray · 6 paper muffin cups
· sieve · wire rack
Ask an adult to help you use the oven

1. Preheat the oven to 190°C/375°F/Gas 5. Put a paper muffin case inside each hole in the muffin tray.

2. Put the butter in a small pan and warm it over a gentle heat until it is melted. Set it aside.

3. Sieve the flour, baking powder, bicarbonate of soda and sugar into a bowl. Make a well in the middle of the ingredients.

4. Mash the banana. Add the egg, milk and melted butter to the banana and stir together until it is well mixed.

Dried fruit

Drying fruit preserves it and allows it to keep much longer than fresh fruit. Fruit can be dried by heat from the Sun or in a machine called a dehydrator. Drying fruit changes the texture and taste of the fruit, making it taste much stronger and sweeter.

5. Cut the woody stems off the figs. Roughly chop the figs and add them to the banana mixture. Stir the mixture well.

6. Pour the banana mixture into the well in the dry ingredients. Mix all the ingredients together until they are just combined. Do not overmix them because the mixture needs to have a rough texture.

7. Using a tablespoon, spoon the muffin mixture into the paper cases. Bake for 20 minutes until the muffins are risen and golden.

8. Wearing a pair of oven gloves, carefully take the muffin tray out of the oven and put it on a heatproof surface. Using a clean tea towel to protect your hands, lift the muffins out of the tin and transfer them to a wire rack to cool. Serve warm or cold.

93

Candy cookies

These pretty cookies are fun to make and delicious to eat. You can be as creative as you like when it comes to decorating them. Spread a smooth layer of icing over each cookie and then decorate them with brightly coloured sweets.

You will need

For 25-30 cookies:
· 175g butter, chilled, plus extra for greasing · 225g plain flour, plus extra for dusting · 125g caster sugar · 1 egg yolk
For the icing:
· 2 tbsp lemon juice · 200g icing sugar, sifted · small sweets to decorate

Extra equipment

· food processor · clear film
· rolling pin · 6cm cookie cutter
· baking sheets · metal spatula
Ask an adult to help you use the oven.

1. Dice the butter.

2. Put the flour in a food processor and put the chilled butter on top of it. Turn on the food processor in short busts until the mixture looks like fine breadcrumbs.

3. Add the sugar and egg yolk to the food processor and process until the mixture comes together in a ball.

4. Sprinkle a little flour onto your work surface then knead the dough until it is smooth. Shape it into a ball and wrap it in clear film. Put it in the fridge for at least 30 minutes to firm up.

Separating eggs

To separate an egg, crack it against the edge of a bowl so that there is a deep crack in the shell. Put your fingers in the crack and pull the shell apart. Keep the yolk in one half of the shell and let the white fall into the bowl. Throw away the part of the egg that you do not need or keep it for another recipe.

5. Preheat the oven to 180°C/350°F/Gas 4. Grease two baking sheets with butter.

6. Sprinkle a light layer of flour over your work surface, then put the ball of chilled dough on top and sprinkle it with a little more flour. Using a rolling pin, roll out the dough thinly.

7. Using the cookie cutter, cut out rounds from the dough, cutting as closely together as you can. Transfer the rounds to the baking sheets, spacing them slightly apart.

8. Bake the cookies for about 12 minutes until they are a pale golden colour. Then use a pair of oven gloves to take the baking sheets out of the oven and put them on a heatproof surface. Slide a metal spatula underneath and lift the cookies onto the wire rack to cool.

9. To make the icing, put the lemon juice in a bowl and gradually stir in the icing sugar until it is smooth and looks like double cream.

10. Spread the icing onto the cookies and decorate them with coloured sweets.

Marshmallow fingers

This rich, squidgy cake is easy to make and requires no baking. Instead, you just need to chill it in the fridge.

You will need
For 8 squares:
- 45g brazil nuts · 85g gingernut biscuits
- 150g milk chocolate · 15g butter · water to melt chocolate · 45g white mini marshmallows · icing sugar for dusting

Extra equipment
- clear film · 2lb loaf tin · plastic bag
- rolling pin · sieve

Ask an adult to help you use the cooker.

1. Tear off a piece of clear film, wider and longer than the loaf tin, and lay it on top of the tin. Press it down so that it covers the base of the tin. Let the extra clear film hang over the edges.

2. Put the nuts on a board and chop each one in half to use later.

3. Put the gingernuts in a plastic bag and twist the top of the bag to seal it. Hold the twisted top of the bag in one hand and use a rolling pin to tap the biscuits to break them up into small pieces. Do not hit them too much or you will end up with just crumbs. If you have a few big bits of biscuit left in the bag, break these up with your fingers. Set the biscuits aside.

4. Pour water into a pan so that it is about 3cm deep. Rest a bowl inside the pan so it hangs above, but does not touch, the water. Put the pan over a medium heat and bring the water to the boil. Then turn the heat as low as it will go so that the water barely simmers.

5. Break the chocolate into pieces and put it in the bowl with the butter. Wait until it is nearly melted, then remove it from the heat and leave it to stand for a few minutes. Stir the chocolate until both the chocolate and butter are completely melted.

Solid chocolate

Chocolate is a solid but it can be melted and changed into a liquid. When the runny chocolate is cooled, it hardens to become a solid again. This type of change is called a reversible change because it can continue to happen.

6. Add the nuts, biscuits and marshmallows to the chocolate and stir until they are well mixed.

7. Tip the mixture into the tin and spread it out in an even layer, pressing down with a spoon. Fold the overhanging clear film over the top so the mixture is covered. Press down on the covered mixture to make sure it is firmly packed in the tin.

8. Put the tin in the fridge for 2 hours until it is firm. Then tip the tin upside down so that the cake falls out. Unwrap the cake and place it on a chopping board.

9. Cut the cake into fingers. Dust the fingers with icing sugar to serve.

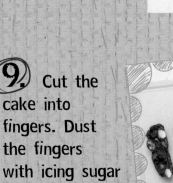

Vanilla cupcakes

Cupcakes topped with creamy icing are easy to make. You can choose whatever colour you like for the icing – yellow, pink, lilac, green or blue will all look great.

1. Preheat the oven to 180ºC/350ºF/ Gas 4. Put a paper cupcake case inside each hole in the cupcake tray.

2. Put the butter and caster sugar in a bowl and beat them to make a pale, creamy mixture.

3. Lightly beat the eggs and add them and the vanilla to the butter mixture a little at a time. Beat until the mixture is smooth.

4. Sieve the flour into the butter mixture and stir until it makes a smooth, creamy mixture.

98

5. Drop spoonfuls of the mixture into the cupcake cases until you have divided the mixture evenly between the cases.

6. Bake the cupcakes for 18 minutes until they are risen and golden. Wearing a pair of oven gloves, remove the tray from the oven and place it on a heatproof surface. After about a minute, transfer the cakes to a wire rack to cool.

7. When the cakes are cool, they are ready to decorate. Put the butter in a medium bowl and beat until it is creamy. Sieve the icing sugar over the butter and add the milk and vanilla. Stir together until creamy. Add 1 or 2 drops of food colouring and stir well to mix.

8. Spread the icing on the top of the cakes, then sprinkle over hundreds and thousands.

Testing if they are cooked

To check if your cupcakes are cooked, gently press the top of a cake with the tip of your finger. If it is cooked, the top will spring back. If it does not spring back, the cakes need to go back in the oven for another minute or two.

Glossary

acid
A substance that contains the gas hydrogen and causes chemical change.
Cream of tartar is an acid.

alkali
A substance that neutralises (balances out) acids. Bicarbonate of soda is an alkali.

bacteria
Organisms that cannot be seen without a microscope. Some bacteria are good
for us but many can make us ill.

balanced diet
This means eating carbohydrates, protein, fat, vitamins, minerals and fibre
in the correct proportions to allow your body to work properly.

calcium
This important mineral is found in dairy foods. It strengthens your bones and teeth.

carbohydrates
Found in starchy foods, such as potatoes, bread, pasta and rice;
carbohydrates provide your body with the energy it needs to work every day.

carbon dioxide
A colourless gas. Carbon dioxide reacts with leavening ingredients to form
bubbles that make dough rise.

fungus
A plant that has no leaves or flowers, which grows on other plants. Mushrooms,
toadstools and yeast are all kinds of fungus.

gelatine
A clear, tasteless substance used to make jellies.

glacé fruit
When fruit is preserved or stored in sugar so that it has a glossy or shiny look.

glacé icing
Icing made from icing sugar and water.

Grant loaves
Traditional wholemeal loaves made by a lady called Doris Grant in the 1940s.

griddle
A metal plate that is heated and cooked on. Drop scones and flatbreads are made on griddles.

hollow
When something is hollow it sounds empty, like there is space inside it.

knead
To pull and stretch dough so that it becomes soft and elastic.

knob of butter
A small amount of butter. If you had to weigh a knob of butter, it would be about 8 g.

leavening ingredient
The ingredient in baking that makes doughs and batters rise. Yeast, bicarbonate of soda and baking powder are all leavening ingredients.

marinade
A sauce used to flavour food. Often food is soaked in the marinade before it is cooked.

mild
Not very strong. Jarlsberg cheese has a mild flavour.

molasses
A sugary syrup used in baking.

nutrients
The goodness found in food that our bodies need to survive.

poppadums
An Indian flatbread that is thin and crispy. Poppadums are usually eaten with dips or chutneys.

protein
Found in meat, fish, eggs, dairy foods, nuts, seeds, pulses, tofu and quorn, protein helps to build muscle and keep other organs inside your body healthy.

pulses
Peas, lentils and beans.

quorn
A type of vegetarian protein.

reversible change
A chemical change that can keep happening.

rye
A cereal used to make bread and biscuits. Rye is similar in colour to wholemeal.

simmer
When a liquid boils, the surface bubbles rapidly but when you turn down the heat, and the surface moves very gently, this is called simmering.

speciality
Something for which an area or person is famous. For example, France's speciality bread is the baguette or French stick and Italy's is the ciabatta or focaccia.

tahini
A savoury dip that is made from sesame seeds.
Tahini is usually used in Middle Eastern food.

tubers
The swollen part of an underground root. Potatoes are tubers.

vitamins
The nutrients that your body needs to grow and develop normally.

well
A hollow or dip made in the middle of a mixture of flour into which liquid is poured.

Index